HARROW
THEN & NOW
IN COLOUR

DON WALTER

*For Elizabeth Cooper, who started it all, and my granddaughter
Emily Bahari-Modaresi, without whose help this book would never
have been finished*

First published 2011

The History Press
The Mill, Brimscombe Port
Stroud, Gloucestershire, GL5 2QG
www.thehistorypress.co.uk

British Library Cataloguing in Publication Data.
A catalogue record for this book is available from the British Library.

ISBN 978 0 7524 6327 8

Typesetting and origination by The History Press.
Printed in India
Manufacturing managed by Jellyfish Print Solutions Ltd

CONTENTS

ACKNOWLEDGEMENTS

In compiling this completely new edition of my earlier book – and, incidentally, my first in colour – I must again thank the many people and institutions who have contributed to my now considerable collection of old photographs, especially the staff of the Harrow Civic Centre Library and the proprietors of the *Harrow Observer*. Inevitably, some of the pictures in these pages came into my possession with no attribution of any kind (sometimes not even a date). For this reason alone, I would be delighted to hear from any reader who can provide further information about them.

ABOUT THE AUTHOR

A lifelong resident of Harrow, Don Walter has channelled his love and knowledge of local history into the creation of ten books, hundreds of local press articles as well as countless lectures and many exhibitions of old prints from his vast collection. In 2005, to mark its 50th anniversary, the Borough of Harrow gave him a special award in recognition of 'generous and unstinting public service'.

INTRODUCTION

Let it be said right away – Harrow is not the place that it was. While this may be cause for celebration to some, for others it is far more a subject for mourning.

Certainly, Central Harrow – as we are now encouraged to call it – could hardly be more different from the one-time hamlet of Greenhill that, around the beginning of the last century, nestled at the foot of the proper town of Harrow, then proudly enthroned on the very top of Harrow Hill.

Hilltop locations, however, have inherent problems. Railways, for example, have to be built on the flat. So first Harrow and Wealdstone on the London-Birmingham Line (1837) and then the first Metropolitan Station (1880) gave a kick-start to significant developments on the lower ground (although, oddly enough, the latter station was – and is still – called Harrow on the Hill!)

Harrow nevertheless remained recognisably Harrow throughout the Second World War and the austerity years that followed. Indeed, it was not until the late 1960s that the very first high-rise buildings appeared on our skylines. Next, in the interests of a more commercially vibrant and viable town, whole streets were gutted to make way for two vast – and, admittedly highly successful – shopping centres.

Their lasting impact, however, was the creation of whole areas with no real identity of their own that could easily be mistaken for, say, Watford or Uxbridge, to quote only two of many possible examples. By contrast, Harrow Hill has now become a little world of its own and, thanks to the care taken of its age-old church, its world-famous school and other fine buildings, it is rarely short of admiring visitors.

Though a book concerned more with buildings than with people tends to hide the fact, perhaps the most significant differences between Harrow 'then' and Harrow 'now' is the ever-broadening ethnic diversity of its residents. As revealed in a profile published as recently as 2006, just over one half of Harrow's population have been recorded as belonging to as many as forty-one different ethnic groups, making the Borough one of only ten local authorities in England and Wales with an 'ethnic minority' majority; moreover, this number is expected to have increased in the next Census findings, thus bringing further diversity to the district's arts and entertainment scene as well as to its shops and restaurants.

Happily, in 2011, all its citizens, whatever their background, can share in a legacy bequeathed by far-sighted twentieth-century administrators: the very significant portion of the Borough's acreage that is still given over to public open space.

COLLEGE ROAD

ANY LIST OF Harrow's most changed roads must surely have College Road near – or possibly at – the very top. The changes, moreover, began at the important entry to what was once the hamlet of Greenhill (now Central Harrow) via the Roxborough Railway Bridge. In the first decade of the last century, the only building of any real substance adjoining the bridge was the popular Roxborough Hotel – even more popular on the day our picture was taken when spectators crowded just about every one of its windows and balconies. What was the source of such excitement? Amazingly enough it was the 1908 Olympic Marathon whose route, beginning at Windsor, took in Harrow on its way to the newly opened White City Stadium.

ELEVEN YEARS INTO the twenty-first century, Roxborough Bridge provides a classic example of town planning gone disastrously awry. Even accepting that by 1989 the old hotel had outlived its usefulness, did its replacement really have to be so vast and featureless a block as Aspect Gate? If that were not bad enough, building subsequently began on an even bigger block – this time of apartments – virtually next door. Worse still, once it had reached ten storeys at its highest point, the general economic climate brought all work to a standstill, leaving the town with a horrendous eyesore at one of its key entry points. Presumably in anticipation of increased traffic, a vast underpass was also created. Relatively few pedestrians, however, seem to make use of it, possibly discouraged by the overgrown state of its so-called gardens and borders.

HARROW MET STATION

FOR ALL THAT Harrow has had a railway station since 1837 (now Harrow and Wealdstone), it was the opening of the Metropolitan Line Station in 1880 that truly put the town on the map. Of necessity it was built on the flat ground of the hamlet of Greenhill; nevertheless it was given the name of Harrow on the Hill since the latter was then the true administrative and commercial centre. More surprisingly, the name has survived to this very day! So important was the Hill community in the Met's early years that the first station, pictured in the 1920s, had its main entrance on the Hill side where cabs could conveniently wait to take city businessmen back to their hilltop homes.

AS THE LOWER ground prospered and the Hill declined in influence, the Met switched its station's main entrance to College Road where it is now somewhat dwarfed by towering office blocks on either side. Since the 1990s, the railway station has been integrated with a bus station servicing an impressive number of routes. Regrettably, this soon became something of a local trouble-spot, a problem only solved by immediate upgrading of its passenger security. Even today, travellers are occasionally startled to see police operating airport-style barriers in an attempt to detect hidden weapons. That their targets are often children of school age makes an unhappy situation even more disturbing.

THE ST ANN'S CENTRE

EVEN THOUGH OUR 'historic' picture (right) was taken some thirty years before Harrow's first shopping centre was to change forever this stretch of College Road, older residents will probably be able to identify each and every one of the buildings it shows. Nearest to the camera (right) is the creeper-clad premises of Heathfield, a popular private school for girls, which happily still prospers, albeit in a new location several miles away in Pinner. Next to the school is the four-square block of the Abbey National Building Society with, beside it, the extensive showrooms of the Grange Furniture Stores. Finally, on the corner of the then Clarendon Road, stood Somertons, regarded by many as Harrow's most fashionable dress shop.

IN 2011 THE same viewpoint reveals only the impressive (or is it oppressive?) entrance of
Harrow's first shopping centre. Opened in November 1987 by no less a personality than Diana,
Princess of Wales, it is called the St Ann's Centre, presumably because it extends all the way back
to the parallel St Ann's Road. Few would describe its frontage as a thing of beauty although, in all
fairness to its architects, they had to incorporate an eleven-storey car park, several of whose levels
can clearly be seen in our picture. Inevitably a construction on this scale meant the demolition
of many well-regarded institutions. Apart from Heathfield School and the other properties
previously mentioned, casualties in the St Ann's Road area included the long-established
Greenhill Laundry and Greenhill School, which first opened its doors to local children in 1860.

CLARENDON ROAD

PERHAPS THE MOST dramatic of all the 'then' and 'now' comparisons in this book is provided by the awful fate that befell Clarendon Road. This was once a pleasantly unpretentious shopping street linking College Road with the end of St Ann's Road where, for over a century, stood a popular public house called The Royal Oak (just visible in our 1950s image). Then, in the 1980s, the building of the vast St Ann's Centre necessitated the demolition of every one of the road's shops

and offices. Even its name sadly disappeared. Where did the name originate? Like so much else in Harrow, it can be traced to the early days of Harrow School and in particular to the Old Harrovian Earl of Clarendon who laid the foundation stone for the 1819–20 rebuilding of Old Schools.

OVER THE LAST thirty years or so what was once friendly little Clarendon Road has become a bleak concrete-and-brick canyon, made even less attractive by road works when our picture was taken. On the right, pedestrians are faced with the winding elevated entry to the multi-storey car park of the St Ann's Centre, and, on the left, the hardly more prepossessing side walls of King's House, which is currently home to a busy Job Centre. They are then but yards away from the wholly brutalist block that houses one of several entrances to the town's second shopping centre. A kind of big brother to St Ann's, it is called the St George's Centre, having opened its doors on St George's Day, 1996.

13

COLLEGE ROAD
POST OFFICE

AS EARLY AS 1895, the existing postal service was obliged to move from the narrow ridge of Harrow Hill to Greenhill where there was still space enough for the acquisition of several small sub post offices. When Greenhill itself continued to expand, a central post office was opened in these handsome – and still-remembered – premises just yards from Harrow Met Station. Here the town's postal requirements were comfortably met from 1914 to the early 1960s by which time the need for an even bigger post office resulted in a total rebuild on the same site. This swallowed up not only the existing premises but also all of its neighbours on the station side.

EARLY THIS CENTURY, a highly ambitious development plan for the station side of College Road forced the existing post office to cross the road to the new premises shown above. For all

that its customer service is spread over some eleven counters, the closing of so many smaller post offices in the Borough means that, at peak business hours, customers are apt to find themselves in a queue that can stretch to the very doors. Worse still, the old premises still stand deserted, neglected and dangerous (if the 'Keep Out' sign is to be believed) while the town awaits a more sensible plan – and a more auspicious financial climate. The resultant eyesore, allied to the number of empty premises in the vicinity, sadly suggests a town on the verge of commercial decline.

ST GEORGE'S CENTRE

THE EMPIRE AND Picturedrome was the very first purpose-built cinema in Greenhill, opening in 1910 at the relatively busy junction of St Ann's Road and Clarendon Road. Surprisingly, it was not a success and was forced to close its doors a year after this picture was taken in 1912. With remarkably few changes to its façade, the building was transformed into Adams (see inset picture), a very large and superior furnishing store. As such, it survived for most of the twentieth century until its site was required for the building of the town's second shopping centre.

IN ONE PARTICULAR, at least, the wheel came full circle when the St George's Centre opened, for, in addition to the anticipated range of shops and restaurants, it offered a nine-screen cinema complex. A success from the start, it probably hastened the closure of the nearby Granada whose

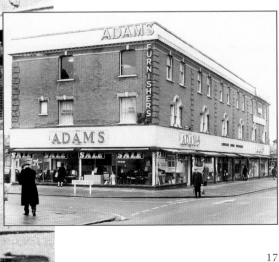

shell has survived in the somewhat unlikely guise of a Gold's Gym. Another survivor even closer to hand is the Royal Oak public house (seen at the right in our 1912 picture), which, after some years as the Rat and Parrot, has recently reclaimed its original name.

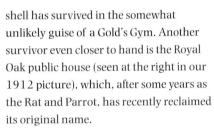

17

ST ANN'S ROAD

FROM THE DAYS when Harrow's limited traffic was largely horse-drawn, St Ann's Road has been known primarily as a shopping street. By the time the picture below was taken (*c.* 1900), there was already a row of well-established businesses along its right-hand side. Most could afford handsome awnings that protected not only their customers but also the sizeable pavement displays allowed in an era when Healthy and Safety by-laws were virtually unknown. Axon's, the ironmongers, for one, had almost as many goods on its forecourt as in its window. Around this time too, the road's junction with Station Road could boast a dairy owned by the local One Hundred Elms Farm, which promised three deliveries of 'pure milk' every day. Lidstone's, a nearby butcher's shop, even had its own on-site abattoir, as testified by early photos of animals being driven through Harrow's streets

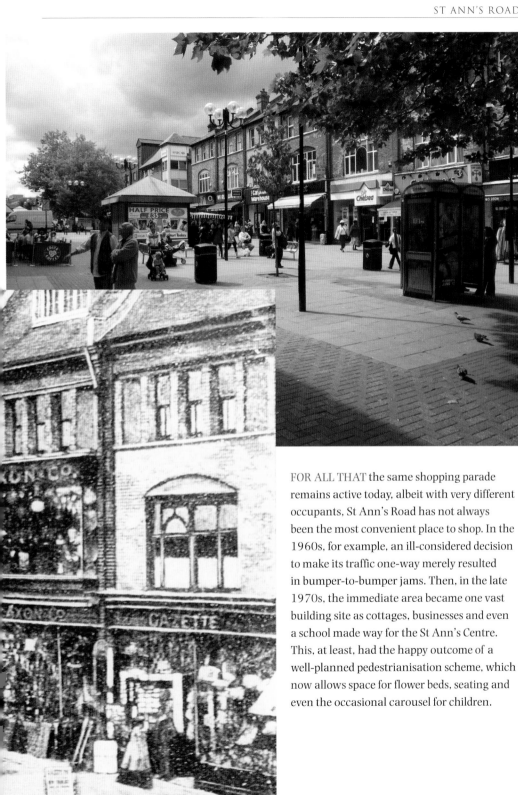

FOR ALL THAT the same shopping parade remains active today, albeit with very different occupants, St Ann's Road has not always been the most convenient place to shop. In the 1960s, for example, an ill-considered decision to make its traffic one-way merely resulted in bumper-to-bumper jams. Then, in the late 1970s, the immediate area became one vast building site as cottages, businesses and even a school made way for the St Ann's Centre. This, at least, had the happy outcome of a well-planned pedestrianisation scheme, which now allows space for flower beds, seating and even the occasional carousel for children.

STATION ROAD – HILL END

STRETCHING ALL THE way from the bottom of Harrow Hill to what was once the totally separate administrative district of Wealdstone, Station Road is undoubtedly one of the longest roads in the Borough. Although Harrow's Metropolitan Line can be accessed from the turning just before the row of one-storey shops, its name is actually derived from the town's first station, now Harrow and Wealdstone, well over a mile away. Much has happened since the photograph on the right was taken in the late 1950s, not least the demolition of the original Harrow Baptist church whose tower can be clearly seen above the shops. Happily, a church of the same denomination can still be found on the same site, but the building itself has been totally remodelled as part of a larger, multi-purpose development.

IN THE PAST fifty or so years, every one of the original buildings on the right-hand side of this stretch of Station Road has been replaced by eclectic examples of twentieth- and even twenty-first- century architecture. There is, however, one notable change for the better. Since April 2010, a red-brick block called Kirkland House has been home to Harrow's first-ever 24-hour central police station (with bright blue doors in place of the old blue lamp). Throughout the author's lifetime, the majority of Harrow's residents have had to travel some distance to find a police station, first to the old cop-shop in West Street and subsequently to a custom-built block in South Harrow, still operational today although no longer offering public access. Equally new to the vicinity is the adjoining Spire House, an apartment block of somewhat curious shape, many of whose windows must offer amazing views – if only of the railway many feet below.

NO. 385 STATION ROAD

IN A ROAD which, as we have seen, has witnessed more than a century of change, the little cottage-loaf shaped building (centre) still stands out. Now No. 385 Station Road, its actual year of building is not readily obtainable although, judging from the long skirts of the passing lady cyclist, the premises were in commercial use well before the First World War. Today the picture's other principal point of interest is the giant directional arrow that points the way to the path (just out of the camera's view) that leads to what was then called the Metropolitan and Great Central Railway Station. At the time a similar sign also existed in College Road directing prospective passengers to that road's station entrance.

A CONTEMPORARY VIEW of the same stretch presents an interesting mix of the old and the new. No. 385, looking remarkably spruce for its age, is now a hairdresser's rejoicing in the name of Wacky Barber, almost as memorable as the neighbouring wine shop, which being a little closer to Harrow Hill calls itself Hill Street Booze. At the time of writing, this part of Station Road was benefiting from an extensive improvement project. A joint venture between Harrow Council and Transport for London, this is a highly welcome combination of pavement renewal and road widening designed to speed the many buses that use this busy road. The work, however, seems to have necessitated the permanent removal of a decorative archway virtually outside No. 385, whose metalwork featured a 'Welcome To Harrow' message.

GAYTON ROAD JUNCTION

GAYTON ROAD, SEEN here in all its leafy splendour
c. 1950 (right), owes its name to the fact that when
Head Master George Butler left Harrow School in
1829, he became the rector of Gayton. Indeed,
such was his local fame that the naming of nearby
Peterborough Road subsequently commemorated
his elevation from humble rector to Dean of
Peterborough. West Harrow, too, has a Butler Road
although this might equally well refer to George's son,
Montagu, who himself became a successful Harrow
head master. For those interested in Harrovian trivia,
other head masters are recalled by such streets as
Vaughan Road, Sumner Road, Drury Road, Hide
Road, Longley Road and Welldon Crescent.

IN RECENT YEARS, Gayton Road has lost much of
the character that made it one of the district's most

desirable addresses. Even the popular lending library built in 1967 is now a boarded-up building site awaiting the start of a development that promises (or possibly threatens) over 380 flats from 4 to 10 storeys in height. Lyon Road, the turning on the left, currently presents an even more dismal picture since several large blocks, orginally built to house local government staff, have been shut down and partially demolished. Should this sad decline drive older residents to drink, it should be said that a public house still survives at the point where the two roads meet. Appropriately enough, it is called The Junction.

THE HARROW
COLISEUM

THOUGH NOT THE first cinema in town, the
Coliseum in Station Road was certainly Harrow's
first true 'picture palace'. Opened in 1920 by
Sir Oswald Mosley, then the town's MP, it was
a highly impressive structure in every way,
distinguished in particular by two rooftop
cupolas. When photographed shortly after its
opening, it could also boast a generous forecourt
for the display of publicity material, but this was
lost when Station Road was widened later the
same decade. Then as now, the shops opposite
were housed in a block known as Bank Buildings
after the branch of Barclays Bank, which,
re-modelled, still stands at the junction with
College Road.

LATER IN ITS career, the Coliseum – or 'The Colley' as it was affectionately known – became the town's first legitimate theatre, hosting many important stage productions before and after their West End runs. It also gave local theatre-goers the chance to see visiting ballet and opera companies, among them the much-loved Carl Rosa. The fact that it was the only theatre for miles nevertheless failed to halt its demolition in 1958 and its replacement by yet another retail outlet, currently a branch of Iceland supermarkets. Sadly, no commemoration plaque was ever erected. Sadder still, over half a century later, Harrow still lacks a proper custom-built theatre of its own.

THE OLD HARROW TECH

ANYONE INTERESTED IN seeing exactly how, and when, significant changes were made to Station Road need only study these three pictures taken over a period of 100 years. Our main picture below *c.* 1910 shows how substantial commercial properties had been developed literally in the front gardens of existing homes, among them an early picture-house whose canopied entrance can be clearly seen. This was the Harrow, later Broadway, Cinema, much patronised by students of the original Harrow Technical College of 1902, whose gables can be glimpsed just behind the telegraph pole. Although the Technical College still stands in our second (inset) image *c.* 1967, it is already dominated by the first of the towering office blocks that changed the local skyline forever.

LAST CENTURY REBUILDING has brought many changes to this busy street, nevertheless any passer-by prompted to look up can still see a few of the rooftops of the original homes transformed into shops to meet the needs of a growing town. As for the Technical College, which began on Harrow Hill in 1887 as a class for 'working boys and girls', it has long since been absorbed into what is now the University of Westminster's Harrow campus on the border of Harrow and Brent. Less fortunate has been the old-established local paper the *Harrow Observer*, which at the time of our old photograph had a vast printing works in the same road. Many years later, it moved across the street to the brick block (centre of our 2011 image) called Trinity House after the paper's new owner, the huge Trinity Mirror Group. A relatively recent rationalisation programme, however, has seen its staff relocated to the Group's Uxbridge premises.

SOPERS/ DEBENHAMS

IN THE YEARS immediately prior to the First World War, the central stretch of Station Road was very much a village on the brink of becoming a town. It had a smithy, a pub called the Marquis of Granby (by the sign, far right), the Church of St John and several substantial residences. Among the latter was the handsome property on the left. Known at various times as Kenmare and the White House, it was knocked down in 1914 in order that a Mr W.H. Soper could build Harrow's first department store. Though pessimists felt it was unlikely that Sopers, as it was called, would weather the privations of war, it survived; not so poor Mr Soper, who, like thousands of others, fell victim to the influenza epidemic that followed the Armistice.

THE SOPERS NAME is still recalled with both respect and affection and, indeed, remained the store's trading name until the 1970s. Only then did it become Debenhams despite the fact that it had been sold as early as the 1920s to a Debenhams subsidiary. In the inter-war years Sopers proved so successful that a major extension was required resulting in a store that could offer over 100 different departments. Later still, a second extension swallowed up the pub next door. Many an ageing resident will recall family outings that began with a shopping spree followed by an in-store tea before enjoying a double bill at the Granada (now a Gold's Gym) just yards away.

ST JOHN'S, GREENHILL

AFTER THE DEATH in 1861 of John Cunningham, vicar of St Mary's, his personal papers confirmed his wish to see a district church established in Greenhill for the benefit of its increasing population, who found themselves at some distance from the old parish church. Accordingly, in 1866, a small though surprisingly ornate church was consecrated in the name of St John at the junction of Station Road and Sheepcote Road. Italianate in influence, its most notable feature

was a stand-alone campanile (glimpsed behind the trees far right). This was topped by a curiously conical roof, which local wags instantly dubbed 'the candle snuffer'.

AS GREENHILL DEVELOPED, the mid Victorian church was quickly outgrown and in 1905 this new and more impressive edifice was built, in part to celebrate the fact that at the end of the century the original St John's had become a parish in its own right. In comparsion with its countrified early days, today's St John's stands at the junction of what have become two of Harrow's busiest roads, Station Road and Sheepcote Road. The latter, in particular, has developed from the rural lane reflected in its name to an exceptionally well-used highway where a rebuilt parish hall now has among its neighbours such present-day institutions as Halfords and a Best Western Hotel.

WEALDSTONE FC GROUND

TWO FEATURES IMMEDIATELY grab the attention in this undated but possibly 1960s aerial view of the Wealdstone end of Station Road. First, and most obviously, there is the old home ground of

Wealdstone Football Club. Secondly, and of almost equal interest, is the large building in the picture's right-hand corner, the only real survivor of the town's once booming cinema business. Opened in 1936 as the Dominion (but now re-christened The Safari and showing exclusively Asian films), this 2500-seater featured the kind of spectacular art deco façade for which its architect F.E. Bromige was famous. Unfortunately, this fell victim to a so-called improvement scheme, which covered up its glories with the dreariest of 'contemporary' cladding – as a close look at the aerial image will reveal.

FOLLOWING THE HIGHLY controversial sale of the Wealdstone Football Ground to Tesco, the site now houses one of the supermarket giant's most successful suburban stores offering seventeen hours of shopping six days a week plus hardly less generous Sunday opening. At the time of writing, the company is again hoping to add a two-storey extension, a new mezzanine floor and an enlarged car park even though public pressure in 2009 forced them to withdraw a similar application. Meanwhile, after some seventeen 'homeless' years, Wealdstone Football Club has successfully established itself at the St George's Stadium in the neighbouring Borough of Hillingdon.

HARROW CIVIC CENTRE AND MOSQUE

FOR MORE THAN half of the last century, the most significant landmark at the Wealdstone end of Station Road was the vast block of Bridge Schools. For all that it looks dismally institutional to contemporary eyes, at the time it was widely acknowledged as a school that consistently gave a decent start to generations of children from the surrounding streets. For some reason, many of these essentially modest roads had been grandly given the names of well-known poets – Shelley, Byron and Wordsworth among them – prompting the whole area to be dubbed 'Poets' Corner'. From the late 1960s, however, the school and most of the roads began to vanish as Harrow's first-ever Civic Centre took shape.

TODAY THE SAME area has not one but two major landmarks: the forty-plus-year-old Civic Centre and, across the road, the virtually complete although still-to-be opened Harrow Central

Mosque and Islamic Centre. Although trees and shrubs have softened its somewhat bleak façade, the Civic Centre now looks very much of its period, which few would regard as a golden age for public building. Ironically, its design was the result of a competition set up after an earlier mock-Georgian plan had been rejected as 'old-fashioned'. As for the mosque, this looks – to an admittedly untutored eye – splendidly traditional and certainly a far cry from the two semi-detached houses next door where local Muslims have been meeting for several decades.

HARROW AND WEALDSTONE STATION

IN THE MID 1830s, when the new London-Birmingham Railway picked Harrow as the first stop outside London, their choice presented them with the very real problem of where to site the station since the only real town at that time was clustered on the very top of the Hill. In the event, they chose the lower ground well over a mile away and thus kick-started the development of the district we now know as Wealdstone. Sadly no pictorial record seems to have survived of this early station. All we know is that in 1912 the highly regarded Gerald Horsley was commissioned to design a brand-new building to which he added a substantial clock-tower from which the picture on the left

was taken. It shows a High Street on the very cusp of development with just a few shops on the right-hand side.

IN MORE WAYS than one, the current view from the station cannot help but sadden. The colourful mural, all 227 feet of it, which borders the station approach actually marks the Borough's greatest tragedy – the 1952 triple train crash that claimed 112 lives and, incidentally, stopped the station clock at precisely 8.19 am. What's more, the immediate area is a mere shadow of its once prosperous self. A misguided decision to take traffic away from the High Street and on to a parallel bypass resulted in such a drop in custom that, in 2011, many of its shops and even its public houses are boarded up. The station itself, however, is remarkably spruce having been subject to a relatively recent refurbishment. This, as a plaque displayed in its street-level concourse records, was completed as a partnership between the railway, English Heritage and the local authority.

39

KODAK LTD

AS EARLY AS the 1880s, Wealdstone was becoming known as Harrow's factory-land as its excellent rail communications attracted one famous business after another. Indeed, by the turn of the century, it was home to, among others, David Allen, the massive print-works that became His Majesty's Stationery Office; Hamilton's Brush Works; Winsor and Newton, the makers of artists' materials; Whitefriars Glass; and, most famously, Kodak. In truth, George Eastman, Kodak's American founder, was seeking more than good communications when he first purchased seven of Wealdstone's acres in 1880. He needed the district's good clean air to ensure that ultra-sensitive photographic procedures could be carried out in a largely dust-free atmosphere. In the 1920s (when our lunch-hour picture was taken) and for many subsequent decades, Kodak was Harrow's biggest employer.

WITH THE IMPORTANT exception of Kodak, most of Wealdstone's major manufacturers have long since departed – some for good. Even Her Majesty's Stationery Office was obliged to close its landmark premises in 1982 and since the early 1990s its vast site in Headstone Drive has housed Harrow's impressive Crown Court. Kodak nevertheless marches on although, given the changes that have overtaken the whole field of image-making, its market dominance is no longer as strong as the glory days when its premises carried a gigantic frieze reading 'You press the button – we do the rest'. Also long gone is the Kodak Hall, once the district's favourite setting for ceremonial events such as the lunch given to Winston Churchill in 1955 when he was made the First Freeman of the new Borough of Harrow.

HOLY TRINITY PARISH CHURCH

IF EVIDENCE WERE needed of the vitality that its many factories brought to early Wealdstone, one need only point to the fact that, by the 1880s, the High Street had gained not one but two imposing churches. First in 1875 was the red-brick Baptist church dominated by a 75ft tower, followed, around a decade later, by the parish church of Holy Trinity. Consecrated in 1886, the latter was largely financed by a handful of the district's wealthier families including the Blackwells of Harrow Weald, forever associated with the famous Crosse and Blackwell brand. It was already a quarter of a century old when its Mothers' Union was pictured setting off on their annual outing, by horse and cart. These vehicles were almost certainly provided by the firm of J. Knott, whose business as carriage builders was located just a few yards from the church.

THOUGH ITS EXTERIOR has remained substantially unchanged, the surroundings of Holy Trinity have altered dramatically in recent years, largely due to the pedestrianisation of the High Street end of Headstone Drive. Since 2002, the year of the queen's Golden Jubilee, the road surface at this point has been enlivened with a dozen colourful mosaic inserts created by pupils of Whitefriars First and Middle Schools. The Wealdstone Active Community, who managed this project, have also been involved in a number of other initiatives designed to regenerate the area. Of these, the most outstanding has undoubtedly been the creation of the Wealdstone Community Centre, an essentially local facility for all ages incorporating a library, youth and community centres and a 'healthy living' café.

THE OLD 'CASE IS ALTERED'

WITH LOTS OF thirsty factory workers in the area, Wealdstone was never short of public houses – of which the curiously-named The Case Is Altered was especially popular, not least for its central High Street location. When the picture below was taken around 1900, it was flanked by picturesque cottages (left) and, just out of view on the right, Garraway's Cab Yard. There can be little doubt that it was the latter that provided the picture's amazing array of vehicles including a particularly elegant wicker chaise (far right). By 1908, however, the cottages had been demolished to make way for the district's first Magistrates' Court whose bench included Harrow Weald resident, Sir William Gilbert of Gilbert and Sullivan fame.

IN 2011, THE case is indeed altered as the original public house is now being prepared for redevelopment and the neighbouring cab yard is home to a branch of Boots. The only remaining landmark is the Magistrates Court of 1908 which, after decades of service as the local police station, is still in police occupation if no longer open to the public. Drinkers intrigued by the origins of the name The Case Is Altered must now travel to Old Redding, Harrow Weald. Here another, even older inn still trades under the name which its proprietors believe originated with the Casa Alta, a Spanish tavern much frequented by British soldiers during the Peninsular Wars of 1808–14.

THE WAR MEMORIAL CLOCK TOWER

EARLY LAST CENTURY, when Wealdstone was small enough for members of its professional classes to be widely known, particular areas were sometimes identified by the names of the most distinguished resident; for example, the junction of High Street and Spencer Road was dubbed 'Doctor's Corner'. The reason lay with Ravenscroft, the large house seen on the right, which was both the home and the surgery of a Dr Butler, the district's Medical Officer of Health, whose son

later followed in his footsteps. Sadly, the peaceful scene here was to change dramatically with the outbreak of the First World War in 1914 when a transit camp was hastily established at nearby Halls Corner (now Fontwell Place). Within days, the streets were to echo to the marching feet (see inset picture) of regular soldiers soon to be transported directly to France – in many cases, never to return.

IF THE HIGH Street/Spencer Road junction had a local nickname today, it would surely be Clock Tower Corner for it was here in 1923 that the local authority built a Wealdstone war memorial that doubled as a clock tower. Incredibly, it was dedicated by Sir Oswald Mosley, the subsequent Fascist leader who, at this less controversial stage of his career, was Harrow's Member of Parliament. Ravenscroft, the so-called doctor's house, has long since been replaced with the inevitable block of flats and the memorial itself has acquired a small but well-tended flowerbed.

ST MARY'S CHURCH, HARROW ON THE HILL

TO SAY THAT Harrow's parish church, St Mary's, has a commanding position is something of an understatement, as King Charles II well knew. Given an uninterrupted view of its spire from his London palace, the monarch dubbed it 'the most visible church' – incidentally providing this author with the title of the history he wrote for its 900th anniversary in 1994. Probably a good deal more of it was visible in the seventeenth century than now or, for that matter, in our *c.* 1928 photograph when sheep grazed on the adjoining Church Fields. As part of his 1847 restoration, the noted architect George Gilbert Scott extended the battlements on the tower along the entire roof-line of the nave. Otherwise the exterior has changed remarkably little with the passage of time.

HAPPILY, THROUGHOUT THE eighty-odd years that separate our photographs, the Church Fields has remained open space. If anything, the view is even more sylvan today as trees and bushes

have significantly grown all around St Mary's churchyard and the buildings on either side. These now include Harrow School's Ryan Theatre, whose presence, it has to be admitted, is by no means as obtrusive as many of its critics feared. It was, in fact, only during the theatre's highly controversial building that the majority of local residents realised that the fields were not council-owned open space but actually belonged to the school; indeed, they were possibly part of founder John Lyon's original endowment.

THE CUNNINGHAM LYCH GATE

WHEN PHOTOGRAPHED EARLY last century, St Mary's lych gate was already one of the best-loved local landmarks. Yet, on its erection some forty years earlier as a memorial to the redoubtable Revd John Cunningham, it received a decidedly mixed reception. Much of the

problem lay with its extravagant Victorian Gothic styling, which was not then to everyone's taste, but which, in truth, was exactly what was to have been expected from the members of Gilbert Scott's practice who were given the design commission. The local paper carped at length about its narrow opening 'taking into consideration the largeness of the congregation'. A correspondent went even further. 'The sooner some of the present fellows get out at night and pull the thing down,' he wrote, 'the better for Harrow.'

OVER ONE HUNDRED years later, the lynch gate remains a favourite background for family (and especially wedding) photographs, despite the somewhat obtrusive presence of a modern lamp post and an invariably overflowing rubbish bin. Sadly the tranquillity provided by its hilltop isolation can become a less welcome eeriness at nights, as is only too well-known to the occupants of the nearby vicarage, whose garden wall is seen on the far left.

ST MARY'S
VIEWPOINT TERRACE

AS EARLY AS 1795, the famous travel book *The Environs of London* was loud in its praises of the view westwards from St Mary's churchyard, which, on a clear day, embraces Windsor Castle – and beyond. In the mid nineteenth century it achieved even greater popularity once it was known that an adjoining tomb had been described by none other than Lord Byron as his 'favourite place' where, as a Harrow schoolboy, he had penned his very first verses. Unfortunately, many visitors wanting to take home a souvenir began chopping little pieces off the tomb. The parish thus felt obliged to set the tomb within a heavy – and rather ugly – metal casing. It was in place when the

picture on the left was taken in 1910 and is still there today.

DECADE AFTER DECADE, 'Byron's tomb' – or, more accurately, that of a certain John Peachey – has continued to attract visitors including King Edward VIII during his years as the Prince of Wales (see inset picture). At the beginning of this century, its importance to Harrow's heritage was recognised by the Harrow Hill Trust who successfully obtained a Millennium Festival Award for the total renovation of the site. Thus today's visitors have the added attraction of a comprehensive information plaque alongside the stone slab recording the full text of the familiar poem that begins 'Spot of my youth'. Such is the exposed situation of the tomb, however, that little more than a decade later, the wording on both stone and plaque is becoming increasingly difficult to read.

HARROW SCHOOL

WHEN JOHN LYON founded the present Harrow School in 1572, he intended it as a free grammar school for local boys but its essentially classical curriculum was largely rejected by the sons

of local farmers and traders. Instead it won almost immediate support from the gentry, whose handsomely-dressed offspring can be seen in this *c.* 1795 print (left). The artist shows the boys at play outside the very first schoolhouse of 1615 which, then as now, was known as Old Schools. The yard in which they are playing also has a traditional name, Bill Yard, since it was here that masters took the traditional roll-call (or bill).

AS LONG AGO as 1820 Old Schools more than doubled its size, its architect achieving balance and harmony by giving both new and old wings identical oriel windows (see above). With its well preserved Fourth Form Room, where the very first classes were taught, and its handsome museum-cum-gallery, this splendid building has become as much a visitor attraction as an educational establishment. Harrow's 800 or so pupils now reside in boarding houses scattered right across Harrow Hill, of which the latest (below) opened as recently as 2010. Called Lyon's House, it is only the second building of its kind the school has built since the Second World War and is sensibly sited in Garlands Lane, off Peterborough Road, some distance from the essentially Victorian buildings that give the school so much of its character.

CHURCH HILL

IF THE EXTERIOR of Old Schools has changed remarkably little since its rebuilding in 1820, the same can hardly be said of its approach via Church Hill. When in 1836 drawing master Thomas Wood sketched the attractive scene shown opposite, Old Schools had a somewhat incongruous neighbour in a tavern called the Crown and Anchor whose upper rooms boasted balconies looking on to the street. Run for decades by the Bliss family, it became known to (wholly illicit) schoolboy patrons as 'the abode of bliss'. The house Wood sketched on the right was Dame Armstrong's, a name deriving from its years as a so-called Dame's House where Harrow boys boarded in the care not of a master but of a respectable local female.

RE-MODELLING OF Church Hill in the last century has resulted in a far more imposing entry to the school with the early inn and nearby shops replaced by attractive terraced gardens (just out of picture). Old Schools now faces a highly imposing war memorial building erected in memory of the 644 Old Harrovians who died in the First World War, a number that, by the end of the later conflict, had grown to close on 1,000. It took some four years to build (1922–1926) as shown by the date worked into its façade on the Church Hill side. The wall of Old Schools projecting on to the pavement also carries a plaque. This recalls the spot where the noted Victorian philanthropist, the 7th Earl of Shaftesbury, was so moved by a pauper's funeral that he resolved to devote his life to the poor.

THE HEAD MASTER'S HOUSE

FOR ABOUT THE first three decades of Harrow School's history, its head masters felt bound by the founder's written statutes to live as well as to work within the confines of Old Schools. In 1670, however, a certain William Horne was allowed to take a house in the High Street both for himself and for the increasing number of so-called 'foreigners' – boys from wealthy homes all over the country who were, of necessity, obliged to board at the school. Almost

certainly, this first house was on roughly the same site as the one seen here in the late nineteenth century, which was itself a replacement for an earlier house gutted by fire in 1838. By the date of our old picture, its status was emphasised by its truly splendid portico bearing the school emblem of a lion rampant – an obvious visual pun on the name of founder John Lyon.

IN EDWARDIAN TIMES Harrow boys could safely stand in the street outside the Head Master's. Sadly, today's ever-escalating traffic has prompted not only a 20mph speed limit over Harrow Hill, but a series of road narrowings, with one sited just yards away from the house's entrance. Another major difference is that the head master himself no longer lives alongside his boys. In 1982, the school decided to build him his own family-sized residence (pictured below) called Peel House after Sir Robert Peel, one of seven Prime Ministers educated at Harrow. Modest in scale, it could hardly present a greater contrast to the original High Street property.

HARROW SCHOOL CHAPEL

FOR OVER 200 years Harrow boys worshipped at the parish church of St Mary's seated in
the nave and, later, in two exclusively school galleries – one built beneath the belfry, the other,
suspended above the north aisle. The boys' restlessness (and worse) during long services
prompted the school to build their own chapel in 1839 although the opposition of Harrow's
vicar, the Revd John Cunningham, meant that services were somewhat unsatisfactorily shared
between church and chapel for several decades. The first chapel (below) was the work of Charles
Cockerell who had earlier rebuilt Old Schools. An essentially modest building, it was little liked –
and quickly outgrown.

The School Chapel, Harrow on the Hill

IN 1854 GEORGE Gilbert Scott was hired by Head Master Charles Vaughan to create a second and more ambitious chapel. Despite being required to construct it in stages around the existing building, Scott produced a notably fine structure, modelled, it is generally accepted, after the Sainte Chapelle in Paris. Since its consecration in 1857, there have been many additions, including both a north and a south transept built in memory of Old Harrovians killed in the South African War. Even the spire, which gives Harrow Hill its famous twin-spire silhouette, was not part of the original chapel being dedicated in 1865 to a long-serving master, 'Billy' Oxenham. Ironically, the latter was always said to have been a stout opponent of any such addition.

HARROW SCHOOL
SPEECH ROOM

UNLIKE GILBERT SCOTT, the idiosyncratic William Burges could never be described as a safe pair of hands, nevertheless Harrow School turned to him for a grand Speech Room to mark the tercentenary celebrations of 1871. Though his design was much admired by the head master of the day, Montagu Butler, Burges' plan is said to have so shocked the original building committee that all but its chairman promptly resigned! This was only the first of countless problems which delayed completion until 1877 and saw further additions being made well into the next century.

As photographed shortly after its opening, Speech Room adjoined a boarding house called Church Hill House, later demolished to make way for the present war memorial block, to which it is now linked.

ALTHOUGH ITS EXTERIOR has been little altered apart from the addition of an imposing statue of Queen Elizabeth I, changes in fashion have seen Speech Room become one of the Hill's most iconic buildings. Over the years, too, it has become increasingly well known as a setting for music and drama, notably the school productions of Shakespeare that closely replicate the staging of the bard's own time. The story behind these productions is a drama in itself, beginning with the Second World War bombs, that, having destroyed all the up-to-date theatrical machinery, left behind little more than a semi-circular performing space. Being akin to Shakespeare's original 'Wooden O', this prompted a whole series of 'authentic' productions which, in turn, did much to inspire the creation of the present day Globe Theatre on London's Bankside.

YEW WALK AND THE RYAN THEATRE

HARROW TOWN HAS long been in the debt of Harrow School for ensuring the survival of acres of open space virtually all around the Harrow Hill, providing it with – in the apt description of the conservationist Harrow Hill Trust – a veritable 'girdle of green'. For many, however, gratitude turned to anger when the school announced plans to build a theatre adjoining the best-loved, most frequented open space of them all, Church Fields immediately below St Mary's. Even less popular was a further plan – ultimately allowed on appeal – to partly finance the theatre by building a modern housing estate to be accessed from West Street. Sadly, residents' fears that this would inevitably mean the loss of cherished viewpoints (as seen in our 1930s picture below) proved wholly justified.

HAVING PROVOKED THE biggest clash between town and gown in living memory, both theatre and housing estate duly arose on possibly the Hill's most sensitive site. A decade or so later, it is only fair to say that the local community still views the results with mixed feelings. The theatre, which is called the Ryan (after the maiden name of the principal donor's wife), is by no means the hulking eyesore many anticipated; indeed, the interior is something of a gem. The design of the houses, however, has won few advocates. Although they have been consciously given a 'period' look, it is hardly the same period as that of the original cottages nearby, resulting in accusations of needless incongruity.

THE OLD KING'S HEAD

FOR CENTURIES, THE King's Head has been known as Harrow Hill's most historic inn. The date of its actual foundation, however, has long been a matter for conjecture. Some time after this image was captured in 1905, its façade acquired the words 'Established 1535'. Yet, curiously enough, the earliest reference to its existence in print is almost 200 years later, in 1706.

ONE SIGNIFICANT DATE is unarguable. In 1992, the King's Head lost its licence following years of mismanagement that had brought undesirable customers (and, not infrequently, the police) to the premises. Its subsequent use as a refugee hostel was always seen as a stop-gap. Like it or not (and very few did), the building's only possible salvation lay in some kind of total transformation. The King's Head, as such, no longer exists. In its place, Harrow Hill now has a residential complex called King Henry Mews in which the carefully restored façade of the old hotel fronts a considerable mews development at its side and rear. As a sop to the many who argued for some continued public use, the local authority reserved a small part of the ground floor and basement for commercial purposes. No one, however, was interested and an official change of use had to be approved before professional tenants could be considered. In the event, an unobtrusive black painted door in the front currently leads into a small cosmetic and dental practice whose specialities include, appropriately enough, 'facial rejuvenation'.

THE GREEN

SITUATED AT THE very heart of Harrow Hill, the little open space opposite the former King's Head has for centuries served as its village green, the setting for both pleasures and punishments (the latter being administered at its stocks and whipping post). From the late eighteenth century, the site has also been used to promote the King's Head by way of a royal portrait suspended from a curiously gallows-like structure. It was certainly the green's only distinguishing feature when the photograph below was taken in 1905. Looking towards London Road, it also shows (left, with

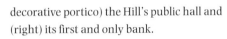

decorative portico) the Hill's public hall and (right) its first and only bank.

MANY OLD BUILDINGS still survive in our 2011 picture, including a substantial part of the shopping parade (left) and the town's first bank (right), currently used as offices. As for the Green itself, it now has the advantage of sponsorship by Stephen J. Woodward, the nearby estate agency, ensuring its regular maintenance and planting. Another attractive contemporary feature is the much-used seat given by the Harrow Hill Trust in memory of the author's wife who worked tirelessly to preserve the Hill. Conscious of the Green's importance to the local heritage, the same organisation currently has well-advanced plans for the renewal of the old 'gallows' structure as a welcome and information point.

THE SHOPPING PARADE

PHOTOGRAPHED AT THE start of the last century, the parade of shops overlooking the old King's Head Green (right) is, above all, a reminder of the days when Harrow Hill was essentially the town's commercial as well as its administrative centre. The parade's other point of interest is undoubtedly its elaborate Victorian architecture which, with its stepped gables and use of patterned red and black bricks, is a conscious echo of the style of several major Harrow School buildings. In such blatant copying we may also detect a hint of flattery since, at the time, a great many of these shops were largely dependent on the patronage of school personnel.

IN 2011, THE shops on King's Head Green remain largely intact although, in the name of modernisation, our town planners inexplicably gave permission to the changes in roof-line all too visible in the contemporary image above. When Central Harrow has so many of its shops boarded up, it is comforting see that the green's premises are all in use and that, among

a preponderance of restaurants appealing as much to visitors as to residents, there is now a small general store. Sadly, an earlier general store on the other side of King's Head Green recently lost its ancillary but much-patronised postal business, leaving the Hill without a post office for the first time since the service was established in the nineteenth century.

THE OLD FIRE STATION

REGARDLESS OF THE fact that in 1838 the whole village had been threatened by a fire that continued burning for many days, it took nearly fifty years before a proper custom-designed fire station was built on a steeply sloping site at the junction of High Street with Byron Hill Road. The slope meant that the firemen's personal quarters were sited below the engine-room so there was no traditional pole for them to slide down whenever the alarm bell sounded. Otherwise the site was eminently suitable, not least for the proximity of the King's Head stables (right), which were able to provide a ready supply of horses for what was, at first, essentially a horse-drawn brigade.

DESPITE HARROW HILL'S ever-diminishing role in the first half of the last century, the fire station continued in use until 1963. Nearly fifty years later, the building is still instantly recognisable although its use could hardly be more different. With remarkably few external changes apart from the removal of the roof-mounted bell, the premises were transformed into the estate agency that currently sponsors the maintenance of the nearby green. A similar conversion for commercial use has also saved several neighbouring buildings such as the Hill's one-time council chambers, now No. 90 High Street. A further interesting survivor (just out of picture) is Harrow's first bank, the London and Counties, later a now sorely missed NatWest branch, currently less conveniently located down the Hill.

THE TOWN WELL

CONVENIENTLY SITED WHERE the High Street meets West Street, the town well was already old when, in the 1580s, nearby resident William Gerard was licensed by a Rectory Manor Roll both to enlarge it and to erect 'a poompe house over the same for the use of all the tenants of the Manor'. Today we can only guess at the size of this early structure but by around 1870 it consisted of little more than a wooden canopy that, from a distance, looked remarkably like the frame of a four-poster bed. Although only a small charge was made for use of the well, it proved too expensive for the very poor who were obliged to take water from local ponds. Over the years,

such practices resulted in a number of deaths from disease, including two well-documented outbreaks of cholera.

WHEN THE WELL was finally shut down, local businessman Thomas Hudson had the happy idea of replacing it with this typically Victorian drinking fountain. Out of use for decades, it has now been restored by the Harrow Hill Trust. Considering that there is a time lapse of some 140 years between the two pictures taken at this point, the external aspects of the view have changed remarkably little. The studio beside the well, once occupied by the photographer Edmund Goshawk, has now acquired a handsome new window while the neighbouring cottages have become a small hotel. It currently adjoins two restaurants, one of which achieved some enviable publicity by calling itself not the Old Harrovian but the Old Etonian; however, no serious offence was taken, a fact endorsed by its continued success.

75

SUDBURY HILL

AS THE AERIAL photograph shows, as late as 1920 there were still many acres of open land either side of Sudbury Hill, which for centuries has been the gateway to Harrow Hill from Wembley. Today the view is of even greater interest in that it shows two 'lost' landmarks. Occupying the centre ground is the sprawling Convent of The Visitation whose claims to our attention include a chapel designed by Giles Gilbert Scott, the hardly less famous son of the architect who gave the hill some of its finest buildings. In addition, in the bottom left-hand corner, the picture shows the graceful Bowden House, which, for much of the twentieth century, served as the Harrow School Sanatorium.

IT WAS ALWAYS unlikely that the open land surrounding Sudbury Hill would remain undeveloped for long – and so it proved. Today Chasewood Park, a truly gigantic development of luxury homes, stands on the former convent site, while slightly lower down the hill is the privately run Clementine Churchill Hospital (lower picture). The former, in particular, was built only after considerable local opposition, climaxing in a public enquiry that permitted the demolition of the convent (by then a nursing home) on the curious condition that the chapel should be deconsecrated and remodelled as a leisure complex! Less controversy attended the hospital's construction, not least because of a design unusually sympathetic to its surroundings. Despite being seriously damaged by fire after the school's departure, the old 'San' could be said to have survived after a fashion, being redeveloped as a number of family-sized homes.

WEST STREET

ONE OF THE Hill's three oldest roads (the others being High Street and Crown Street), West Street had a full complement of shops and even a public house *c.* 1907. Virtually all have long since vanished including Masseys (left), which somewhat curiously combined the roles of funeral director and newsagent! The substantial building on the right was then the Mission House of St Mary's, built in part for the convenience of older residents who found it difficult to climb the steep hill to the parish church. At West Street's lower end, at the junction with Nelson Road, stood The Cricketers, a name undoubtedly chosen for the pub's proximity to Harrow School's cricket pitches.

TODAY WEST STREET still has much to offer the visitor, especially those who know something of its history. The building that once housed The Cricketers is now a private house but its walls still boast the panels where advertising material was once displayed. The 1884 Mission House also looks much as it has always done although, for several decades, it has been used as a factory for plastic components. West Street visitors should not fail to take the adjoining public footpath, not least for the glimpse it quickly affords of a timber-framed building within the factory's grounds, which just happens to be Harrow On The Hill's second oldest building. Dating from *c.* 1350, it was built as a court house to dispense summary justice on the nearby Church Fields which, for centuries, were home to the town's regular fairs and markets.

MIDDLE ROAD

AROUND A HUNDRED years ago, Middle Road was a highly popular address
as much for its shops as for its houses. At a time when so many men proudly
sported beards – or, at the very least, handsome moustaches – Bentley's
Hairdressing and Shampooing Rooms (right, with 'Shaving' sign outside) would
rarely have lacked for custom. Equally well patronised were the family butcher,
J. Fox (nearest camera), the local sub post office of the Harrow Postal Service
and The White Horse public house. The road could also boast several attractive
properties, among them Roxeth Mead (just out of the picture), which in 1856
its newly widowed and impoverished owner, Hebe Prior, had been obliged to
turn into a preparatory school.

PRESENT-DAY MIDDLE Road is almost wholly residential, as testified by the
large number of family cars obliged by a dearth of garages to be parked in
the street. The only truly commercial enterprise is The White Horse, which,
having undergone a total rebuild during the twentieth century, still trades on
its original site. Roxeth Mead is another survivor although, in recent times, the
house has been redeveloped and its grounds used for building the small estate

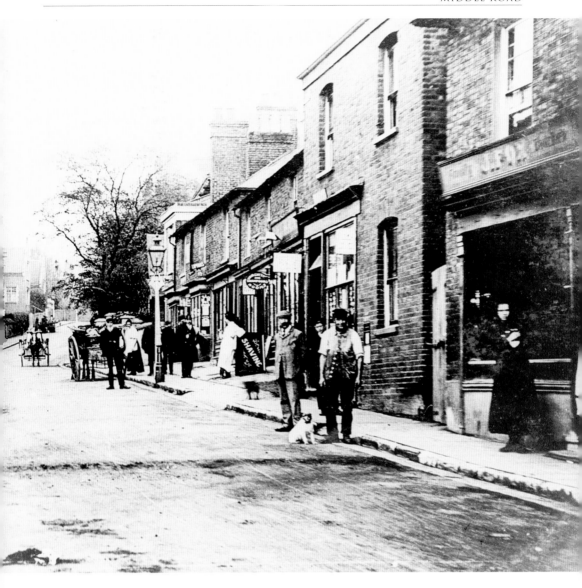

known as Chartwell Place. The school, however, continues, having moved to a neighbouring property. For those with a liking for idiosyncratic Victorian domestic architecture, Middle Road will always be associated with E.S. Prior who not only designed the attractive terrace (far left) but also turned an old inn further up the road into The Red House, now used by the John Lyon School.

THE JOHN LYON SCHOOL

NOW A TOTALLY separate foundation in its own right, The John Lyon School can nevertheless show a direct descent from the English Form opened in the mid nineteenth century by Harrow School's head master Charles Vaughan. Financed from Vaughan's own pocket, it was his personal answer to well-justified criticisms that local lads could no longer afford Harrow School itself. In this modest guise, it struggled to survive for years until the Public Schools Act of 1868 decreed that it should be given a new schoolhouse and a better endowment. A suitable site was then found in Middle Road where the building, photographed here at the turn of the last century, finally opened in 1876.

JUST LIKE HARROW School, The John Lyon School has subsequently had to spread itself over a considerable area in order to grow and prosper. Quite apart from the very substantial block to be glimpsed behind the original building in our 2011 photograph, virtually all the land bordering the junction of Middle Road and Crown Street now houses not just classrooms but all the other facilities a modern school demands. Thanks to notably sensitive planning, much of it is discreetly hidden from view by a singularly beautiful old wall that once bordered a property called Oldfield House whose equally splendid gateway has also been retained. The modern school has also spilled across Middle Road to The Red House, a former inn later converted into a home for members of his family by the distinguished architect E.S. Prior.

THE GROVE FIELDS

THE GREEN SLOPES of the Hill were snowy white when this picture was shot on Grove Fields in February 1969. Once one of the Borough's greatest view points, it takes its name from The Grove, now a Harrow School boarding house, at the very top of the slope. Rebuilt on several occasions, this still-grand mansion first attracted the attention of the playwright Richard Brinsley Sheridan during his schooldays at Harrow in the 1760s. Little more than a decade later, by which time he

had achieved early fame with *The Rivals* and *The School for Scandal*, he took a lease on the property, making it his family home for many years.

GROVE FIELDS IS happily still a public open space although the views it now affords are strictly limited by late twentieth-century building. Where once one could see the far-away chimney of the Kodak factory and the countryside beyond, these distant prospects are now obliterated by the towering office blocks in Lowlands Road, among them Technology House on the corner and, just a few yards away, the aptly-named The Heights. The only piece of open land still visible is the tiny Lowlands Recreation Ground and even this has recently been under threat of development. Just out of camera-view on the right, however, two survivors of an earlier era remain: the Georgian villa of Lowlands and the 1912 block of the Harrow Girls' County School, both of which now form part of the extensive campus of Harrow College.

SOUTH HARROW STATION

IT IS ENTIRELY appropriate that our first reference to South Harrow should concern the railway station opened in 1903. Until then, this part of Harrow was invariably known as Roxeth (or 'good old Roxey'), a name that is documented as early as AD 845. The bosses of what was then the District Line, however, felt that South Harrow was easier both to spell and to pronounce. Nevertheless, as a sop to local traditions, they allowed the original platform signs to read 'South Harrow – for Roxeth and Northolt'.

THE OLD STATION survived until 1932 when it was rebuilt in the now classic London Transport style of the period. Almost eighty years later, the actual line has changed – it is now the Piccadilly – but much else is as it has always been; in particular, an intimidating flight of steps that has to be mounted before either platform is reached! The few additions include a small adjacent bus station and a large car park, the latter having been built in the grounds of the first station house. Home to the stationmaster and his wife, this original building can clearly be seen at the end of the up platform in the photograph above.

ROXETH GASWORKS

COMPARED WITH THE genteel Harrow Hill, nineteenth-century Roxeth was essentially a working-class community: a great many Roxeyites either worked directly or indirectly for Harrow School or were employed at the gasworks, which opened in Northolt Road in 1855. Its opening, in fact, was greatly welcomed for, against all odds, its proprietor, John Chapman, was able to keep his promise to supply parts of the town with gas within a period of just six months. Much later, however, much good will was lost when the company ignored widespread opposition to build a huge gasometer. This towering structure remained in place long after it had served

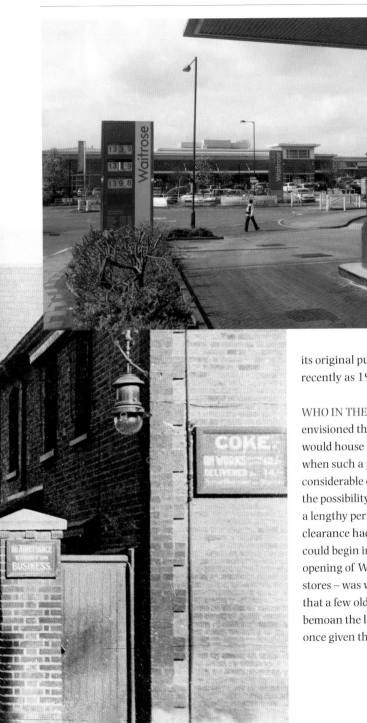

its original purpose, being taken down as recently as 1980.

WHO IN THEIR wildest dreams could have envisioned that one day the gasworks site would house a supermarket? In truth, when such a proposal was first discussed, considerable concern was expressed about the possibility of site contamination and a lengthy period of both cleansing and clearance had to elapse before construction could begin in the 1990s. Though the opening of Waitrose – and other big-name stores – was widely popular, it was inevitable that a few older folk would continue to bemoan the loss of old buildings that had once given the area much of its character.

NORTHOLT ROAD, SOUTH HARROW

IF THE HILL end of Northolt Road seems unusually busy in our 1906 photograph (right), the reason would seem to lie with the large marquee that has been erected on one of the fields then belonging to Grange Farm. Here, according to contemporary press accounts, Roxeth folk attended a highly successful Baptist Mission, a circumstance which may also explain why everybody in the picture seems to be wearing their Sunday best. The same site was also used for the first meetings of the Roxeth Salvation Army who in 1886 opened their own premises on nearby Roxeth Hill.

NORTHOLT ROAD IS yet another of the Borough's oldest thoroughfares that would be totally unrecognisable to anyone who left the area even as recently as the 1960s. Apart from the British Legion Club (whose clock can be glimpsed above) virtually all of its mid twentieth century buildings have now disappeared. Where once there were parades of little shops and houses, there is now an eclectic mix of local authority housing and health and childcare facilities whose

construction swallowed up the whole of Alma Road with its picturesque two-up, two-down
cottages. More recent redevelopment has seen the opening of a Eurotraveller Premier Hotel and,
on the opposite side, the loss of the Timber Carriage public house. The latter was itself a rebuild of
an earlier, more modest inn with an equally modest name – the Timber Cart.

ROXETH SCHOOL

ERECTED IN 1851, this lovely old Victorian schoolhouse still forms part of today's Roxeth First and Middle Schools. The original Roxeth School, in fact, is even older, having been founded – albeit on a different site lower down the Hill – as long ago as 1812 by the recently appointed vicar of Harrow, the Revd John Cunningham. His little school's opening did much to ease the existing bad feeling between many of his parishioners and the governors of the elitist Harrow School over what the former saw as a betrayal of its founder's intentions to run a free grammar school for local boys.

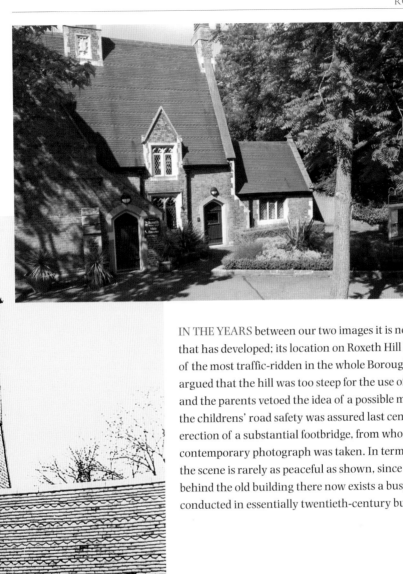

IN THE YEARS between our two images it is not just the school that has developed; its location on Roxeth Hill has become one of the most traffic-ridden in the whole Borough. Since the police argued that the hill was too steep for the use of traffic lights and the parents vetoed the idea of a possible murky underpass, the childrens' road safety was assured last century by the erection of a substantial footbridge, from whose lowest level our contemporary photograph was taken. In term time, of course, the scene is rarely as peaceful as shown, since immediately behind the old building there now exists a busy modern school conducted in essentially twentieth-century buildings.

THE OLD COTTAGE HOSPITAL

FOR THE GREATER part of the twentieth century, Roxeth Hill was known to locals as Hospital Hill. This affectionate naming followed the building in 1906 of Harrow Cottage Hospital although, even earlier in the 1860s, the self-same hill had seen the conversion of two cottages into a very modest nine-bed facility. Designed by the highly regarded Arnold Mitchell, the Edwardian building was frequently dubbed 'the most perfect little hospital in England' but, ultimately, proved just too small for a town that had grown beyond all expectations. From 1970 onwards, most of its services were taken over by the vast Northwick Park Hospital in Watford Road. Inevitably, when its doors finally closed in 1998, it left an enormous site to the doubtful mercy of modern developers.

IN THE EVENT, the redevelopment of this key site went to the relatively sympathetic Barratt Homes, who, from the start, proposed to retain and restore Arnold Mitchell's original core building as luxury apartments (inset). Given the importance of the site, a public enquiry was ordered in 2003 which resulted in some inevitable compromises – virtually no reduction in the scale of the project but some helpful 'second thoughts' about the buildings' height and overall design. What might have been a major stumbling block – a covenant on the former nurses' home requiring its continuance as a hostel or single-family residence – was also sensibly overcome by the creation of a brand-new YMCA hostel now called Roxeth Gate.

Other titles published by The History Press

One Man's War: An Essex Soldier in World War Two

BILL DAVIES

A veteran of D-Day, Ron Davies joined the TA before war began and was called up as a tank gunner or 'Bombardier' with the Essex Yeomanry, but D-Day was his first experience of action. This book follows the training and build-up to D-Day, covers the invasion minute-by-minute, and carries on through the Allied Push through France, Belgium and Holland. Ron's story continues with the regiment's heartbreaking round of duty at Belsen and following that their continuation to the Baltic Coast.

978 0 7524 4517 5

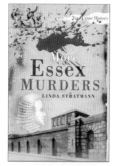

More Essex Murders

LINDA STRATMANN

From the pretty villages, rural byways and bustling market towns of Essex come ten of the most dramatic and tragic murder cases in British history. Brutality, passion, jealousy, greed and moments of inexplicable rage have led to violent and horrifying deaths and, sometimes, the killer's expiation of the crime on the scaffold. This chilling follow-up to *Essex Murders* brings together more true cases, dating between 1823 and 1960, that shocked not only the county but also made headline news across the nation.

978 0 7524 5850 2

Paranormal Essex

JASON DAY

Join journalist, broadcaster and paranormal investigator Jason Day on a tour around one of England's oldest and most paranormally active counties. Visit the site of the 'Most Haunted House In England' at Borley, encounter the mysterious Spider of Stock, witness an RAF pilot's shocking near miss with a UFO over the skies of Southend, and find out how the infamous 'Witchfinder General' served as judge, jury and executioner in Manningtree. *Paranormal Essex* will delight all lovers of the unexplained.

978 0 7524 5527 3

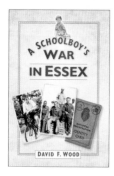

A Schoolboy's War in Essex

DAVID F. WOOD

Although only children at the time, the Second World War had a permanent effect on the schoolboys who lived through the conflict. Watching a country preparing for war and then being immersed in the horrors of the Blitz brought encounters and events that some will never forget. Now in their seventies and eighties, many are revisiting their memories of this time of upheaval and strife for the first time. In this charming book, David F. Wood recalls his days as a schoolboy in Essex.

978 0 7524 5517 4

Visit our website and discover thousands of other History Press books.
www.thehistorypress.co.uk